Scrum For Newbies

The Amazingly Simple, Plain English Guide To Getting Started With Scrum

by Jeremy Wilson

Table of Contents

Introduction 1

Understanding Scrum the Easy Way 3

    The Steps and Key Concepts of Scrum 5

Discover Scrum: Your Scrum Dictionary 12

Your Ultimate How-to-Use-Scrum Guide 20

    Quick and Simple Ways to Understand Scrum: Basic Scrum Principles 20

How to Implement Scrum in 6 Easy, 20 Minutes-or-Less Steps 26

How to Rescue a Project with Scrum: The Delicate Art of Adopting Scrum And Saving Projects 29

    Talk About the Benefits of Using Scrum, Not How Cool It

Common Scrum Mistakes to Avoid At All Costs 32

Conclusion 35

Introduction

Thanks and congratulations for downloading "Scrum For Newbies: The amazingly simple, plain English guide to getting started with Scrum."

With this guide, you'll be able to grasp what Scrum is REALLY about in less than an hour... it's exactly what you need to get started applying Scrum to your projects.

It shows you logically, using terms you understand, how to apply Scrum to a real business.

You get practical notes on how to implement Scrum -- plus pitfalls to watch out for.

You'll find the insights helpful before taking the course. And for experienced professionals... it's a great refresher after training.

For Scrum beginners, this guide will ensure you're no longer in the dark during project review meetings.

Here's what we'll be covering:

- The steps and key concepts of Scrum
- How to approach Scrum in 20 minutes or less
- Quick and simple ways to understand Scrum basics
- What is a Scrum master -- and how are they different from a project manager?
- How to rescue a project with Scrum
- The true meaning of Scrum
- Common Scrum mistakes to avoid at all costs

Thanks again for downloading this book, I hope you enjoy it!

Let's take a step back and look at the big picture.

Where does Scrum fit into your life?

Well, almost every project demands that many different elements come together to achieve one goal.

This is true even when applied to a business as a whole. Even though a business is segmented into various departments -- sales and marketing, human resources, management, development, etc. – everybody in the business, every team, and team member in that business works towards the achievement of one or more goals as outlined by the company.

In other words, regardless of the scope of a project, you need to coordinate between different teams working towards the same goal. Without coordination, it all falls down!

So, how do you go about doing this coordination?

There are lots of ways – but one of the best and most effective is Scrum.

If this is your first time taking a dip in the Scrum pool, I'm sure you're very curious. You might even be somewhat perplexed at how to properly implement Scrum. Well, you're in luck. This book will teach you everything you need to learn and know to start using Scrum like a pro.

Let's get started.

Understanding Scrum the Easy Way

If this is the first time you've been introduced to Scrum, I've got some bad news for you: you've been missing out on a truly amazing concept. The good news is it won't take you long to start applying it to your work.

To put it into managerese:

Scrum is an incremental methodology popularly deployed in software development for managing product development.

Moreover, Scrum is a lightweight framework that enables small and close-knit people to develop a complex product.

Scrum is applicable to any project featuring complex requirements, aggressive deadlines, and a degree of exceptionality. In a Scrum framework, project development moves forward via series of phases called sprints, with each sprint taking two to four weeks.

In other words, Scrum is a "set of rules" (a framework) for doing complicated things in a dynamic way, while (hopefully) achieving the best possible result.

Probably the most important part of the Scrum concept is the "sprint." A **Sprint is just a "development phase" where the Development team creates something useful... before stopping to come up for air and make sure everything is on the right track.**

What makes Scrum special is the focus on "empiricism." Empiricism is a fancy way of saying that the only way to know something is to have experienced it... and, by the way, you should only make decisions based on what you know.

Therefore, in Scrum, the basic idea is to make decisions based on things you've experienced, not based on fuzzy projections or guesswork.

Furthermore, by taking an incremental and iterative "do something, then check your work" approach, Scrum controls risk and makes things much more predictable.

As a management tool, Scrum has gained a lot of traction in the technology field. Here it's a popular tool for coordinating and managing application and software development.

But, make no mistake. Just because Scrum is used for technical tasks does not mean that it, itself is an overly technical tool. In fact, you can easily adapt its tools and practices to nearly any kind of project.

So, where do you start?

To completely understand the Scrum framework and build better projects, I'd suggest you begin by understanding the key Scrum concepts and rules. Let's take a closer look at these.

The Steps and Key Concepts of Scrum

The defining feature of Scrum is its interactivity. With Scrum, project development is split up into many different phases. Each of these phases is set up so that it results in a product – either one that's ready for market or a prototype.

The idea behind this structure is that it makes feedback easy. After each phase or step is completed, the finished or prototype product goes to the customer. (The customer might be an internal customer, like a manager or team. Or, they might be a customer in the conventional sense of the word, like a paying client or a market research focus group.)

At this point, the customer gives feedback on the product. Based on this feedback, the project team goes back and looks for any problems in their work – or any issues with the plan as a whole – and then makes changes if necessary.

In order to have your project follow the core Scrum steps, it should have the following elements, or "core values":

- A product owner: His or her role is to represent the interests of the end user.

- A Scrum master: A Scrum master coordinates the entire process and makes sure that Scrum is utilized and implemented correctly.

- A Scrum team: A Scrum team creates the product and is responsible for tasks like programming, testing, analyzing, or any similar goal.

Now that you know the key values, let's go on to the core steps involved in a Scrum project.

Step#1: Product Backlog Creation

Basically, the product backlog is a directory or list of features that need to be applied, created, or implemented during the project.

The product backlog is organized according to the priority of each task or feature. However, in Scrum we don't refer to them as "tasks" or "features."

Scrum is very user focused, and the goal is to create a product (even if that product is actually a service) which fits the user's needs and desires. Therefore, the items on the product backlog are called the "user story."

Each User Story has a unique ID, to make referring to it later easier.

Here's an example of a product backlog.

Id	User story
a-001	I Being a manager, reserve the option of adding, deleting and editing tasks to manage the employee's tasks. (1 story point, demo via web GUI)
a-002	I being a manger, would like to have the ability to change the period and the beginning date of initial projects via drop and drop and add new tasks (3 story points, demo via web GUI)
a-003	I being a manger, would want to come up with two types of employees; 1- Full-time task 2- Part time task (2 story points, demo via web GUI)

Sample product Backlog table 1

6

Every user story "line item" in the product backlog should have the following elements:

- Importance of a user story- You can use any number you want while creating this step. For example, in our table, we have used a-001 for the first user story

- Initial estimate- This describes the overall amount of work. Usually measured in story points

- How to demo- This describes how the working product should be demonstrated

Step#2: Sprint Planning and Sprint Backlog Creation

For this step, start out by setting the duration of your sprint.

A shorter sprint will result in a quicker product release. And, a faster product release means the working report will be done sooner. The customer feedback will be received sooner, and any bugs or errors will be found faster.

On the other hand, longer sprint durations give your sprint team more time to work That lets them work more cautiously and carefully, and lets them complete more complex and involved tasks.

Therefore, it's up to you to choose the optimal sprint time.

Scrum "rules" state that sprints should be no more than two weeks, in general.

The other key thing about the sprint stage is team member and stakeholder collaboration.

What do I mean? Simple. The product owner, for example, is in charge of determining the significance of a given user story – whether or not it's worth implementing a given feature request, or what its priority is.

The Scrum team, on the other hand, is responsible for estimating the amount of labor involved.

The product owner may also choose the most pressing user story from the backlog, and leave the team to decide how to work out the task.

Now, moving forward, before starting a given sprint, the scrum team needs to create the sprint backlog, choosing the user stories which they plan to finish in the current sprint.

The number of user stories chosen, and the number of "story points" involved, determines how much time will be allocated to each of them during the evolution stage. The goal is for the Scrum team to complete all the stories in the given amount of time.

Step#3: Working On the Sprint: Scrum Meetings

Once you choose the current step's user stories, the development process starts.

A crucial feature of this stage is the regular day-to-day Scrum meeting.

The main objective for these meetings is to get accurate information about the status of the current project. In addition, in the course of these meetings, each member should update the others concerning the task he/she has finished, the task to complete next, and the problems encountered in the last task.

There's usually a task board, which is used to follow the progress of current work.

This task board is a central feature of most Scrum meetings. Task boards are basically big cards featuring written names of certain user stories and a set of tiny sticky note descriptions of single duties used to implement the story.

These cards are kept in order of their importance.

When the work that's part of a given task begins, the matching sticker is shifted to the To-do field next to the in-progress field as depicted in the figure below.

After the work is completed, the small sticker can be shifted to the testing field. When it's tested successfully, it is moved to the done field.

Below is a Scrum task board example.

Stories	To Do	In Progress	Testing	Done
Task #1	Task #2 Task #3 Task #6	Task #7 Task #9	Task #8	Task #16 Task #17
New task	Task #10 Task #11	Task #12	Task #13 Task #14	Task #15

After the Scrum meeting, the Scrum team gets a burn-down chart. This chart shows you the number of uncompleted tasks. This makes it much easier to control the development process. As a result, the chart should be updated after every attended meeting.

In the example below, x –axis indicates the outstanding working days while y-axis shows the general number of story points in the present stage.

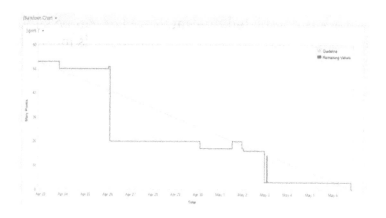

Step#4: Testing and Product Demonstration

Given that the ideal outcome of each sprint is a working product, the process of testing is crucial.

At the same time, since testing doesn't necessarily contribute to forward progress, you don't want to spend more time than necessary on this stage.

There are various ways to minimize the length of the testing process. For instance, you can choose to reduce the overall number of user stories. This will lead to a decreased number of possible bugs.

Alternately, you can incorporate QA engineers into the team. This makes it possible to do QA during development – hopefully meaning that bugs get found and fixed early, before they can "grow" into major problems that need major fixes.

At the end of each sprint is the product demonstration. The Scrum team should write an working report and demonstrate the results of their hard work.

At this point, the stakeholders can decide on any necessary changes to the project.

Step #5: Retrospective and Next Sprint Planning

The main aim of a retrospective is to talk about the results and decide how to advance the development process for the upcoming step.

The Scrum team decides what was successful and not successful while undertaking the current task, and what to be improved for the next iteration.

Once the means of improvement is decided on, the team can focus on planning for the next sprint.

What is a Scrum master and how are they different from a project manager?

Contrary to popular belief, the roles of a Scrum master and a project manager are different. Try not to confuse them!

A project manager is a leader, planner, decision maker and someone who manages the team and the project. He or she is the person accountable to the business in terms of achieving project objectives.

The role of the Scrum master is more that of a coach and facilitator.

The Scrum master's role is to interface between the project and the customer. A Scrum master does not manage the team that produces the work. Rather, he or she supports the product owner, coaches the team and ensures that the Scrum processes are properly followed.

As you may have noticed, the Scrum framework has a few vocabulary words unique to Scrum.

This can be confusing to someone who has never used Scrum before.

Therefore, before we move on to Scrum implementation, let us look at some of the most common and important Scrum terms.

Discover Scrum: Your Scrum Dictionary

In the Scrum framework, there are many different terms used to describe the various Scrum processes.

As a beginner, some of these terms might leave you feeling like you're in the dark. It's crucial that you understand these terms before we go any further.

Burn Down Charts

Burn down charts show the amount of work remaining.

The chart should be drawn in a neat and systematic way. In general, on a burn down chart the y-axis indicates the remaining work and x-axis indicates the time required to complete the work.

Scrum books are used to define the sprint burn down chart, and where to view daily progress.

Daily Scrum Meeting

In a Scrum framework, there are fifteen-minute meetings, happening daily. In these meetings, every member of the team has to answer the following questions:

"From the previous meeting, which task have I carried out?"

"Before we gather for the next meeting, what will I do?"

"In the overall progress of the team, am I performing poorly?

"What is the cause of any poor performance?"

Scrum Master

Like we discussed earlier, the Scrum master makes sure everyone follows the basic Scrum procedures, and helps interface between team and customer.

For example, a Scrum master might step in to ensure that members of the team call for a meeting to discuss any problems that may have gone outside the team's constraints.

He recommends the time the meeting should happen and under which conditions the meeting should start. For example, "this meeting will start early tomorrow morning after all members of the team arrive."

Also, the Scrum master is in charge of helping people outside the team understand what helps the team – and what doesn't. Is it really helpful for the customer to ask for detailed status updates every morning, or is that not really helping anyone get anything done?

At the same time the Scrum master doesn't really "represent" any particular party. They help the product owner (or customer) by making sure things go smoothly. They help the Scrum team by coaching them and removing impediments.

And they also help the organization as a whole, by facilitating Scrum adoption and helping the Scrum team interface with the organization as a whole.

Impediments

In a Scrum framework, anything that hinders team members in the performance and accomplishment of their duties is an impediment.

Every team member who has encountered any impediment should report it in the Scrum daily meeting.

After reporting, the Scrum master will be in charge of ensuring that the impediments are resolved.

In case the issue can't be settled during the Scrum meeting, the Scrum master arranges a sidebar meeting to take care of it.

Product Backlog

The product backlog represents the project requirements. It's a constantly changing document, evolving as development continues.

Basically, in the backlog the requirements are articulated as a list of prioritized items. This list includes both non-functional and functional requirements of the customer as well as technical requirements that the team has generated.

It's the duty of the product owner to ensure the product backlog is properly prioritized. In the sprint planning meeting, product backlog items should be moved to the sprint backlog depending on the product owner's priorities.

Product Backlog Item (PBI)

In Scrum, PBI is a small section of work that should be done by the team in single sprint iteration. The backlog-items may consist of one or several tasks.

There might be several product backlog items per sprint. The product backlog item, therefore, is not to be confused with the Sprint Backlog. (The Sprint Backlog is the set of product backlog items chosen for the sprint.)

Product Backlog Item Effort

In Scrum, some prefer estimating effort in terms of the days it will take to complete product backlog-items.

Some choose the less concrete-sounding estimated units, which might include function or story points.

The benefit of estimation units is that they make it clear clear that the effort estimated for the product-backlog-item is not an estimate of duration. They are just uneven guesses, which should not be confused with the actual working hours.

Product Burn-Down Chart

The product burn-down chart is a big picture chart that shows the progress of a project. It indicates the level of work yet undone at the start of every sprint. Below is an example of a product burn-down chart.

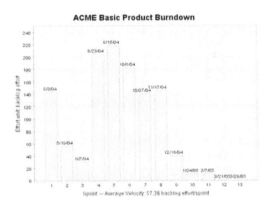

Product Owner Role

In Scrum, one person should have the final authority that represents the customer's interest in requirements and backlog prioritization.

This person is the product owner. Ultimately, the job of the product owner is to maximize the product's value.

The product owner is always one person, and never a committee – even if the product owner represents the interests of a committee. They are the sole person in charge of the product backlog, and the team is not allowed to act on anything anyone else says.

The product owner should be in close contact with (and possibly part of) the team, especially during the sprint review meeting and sprint planning meetings.

Release

Release occurs when a product moves from the Scrum team into use by customers. This usually happens when the product owner decides an increment or Product Backlog Item is "done" and usable.

One word of caution – everyone needs to understand what "done" actually means. When is done really done? The answer is different for almost every situation, but it needs to be understood by everyone.

Also, as the team and development effort matures, it's assumed that the definition of "done" will also mature.

Release Burn Down Chart

This big picture chart shows the release progress. It indicates the amount of work yet undone at the start of every sprint containing a single release. Its scale is a single release. Despite that, a product burn down chart covers all releases.

Sprint

The sprint is the "heart" of any Scrum process.

It's a window of time – ideally less than two weeks, sometimes as long as month – during which the development team creates the "product increment."

In other words, it's the period of time where the development team tries to produce a potentially releasable, useable, and "done" (for whatever definition) sub-product (the "increment").

You can think of Sprints as mini-projects.

Sprints start with a single day sprint meeting. At the end of every Sprint, a review sprint meeting occurs.

Through the sprint, the team should not be disturbed with any additional work. This ensures full commitment and concentration in that sprint.

Sprint Backlog

The sprint backlog defines the work to be done during that sprint. It's just the Product Backlog Items chosen for a given Sprint, ideally alongside a plan for delivering them and realizing the goal for that Sprint.

The development team changes the Sprint Backlog as the Sprint progresses, adding new work as required and removing any items which turn out to be unnecessary. Only the development team can change their Sprint Backlog during the sprint.

The Sprint Backlog, when done right, is a real-time picture of the work the team is planning to accomplish.

Sprint Burn down Chart

This graph shows teams the position they are at in terms of carrying out product-backlog-items – in other words, towards attaining sprint goals. The X-axis indicates the number of days in that particular sprint while y-axis shows the effort remaining.

Over time, the chart drops to zero as the sprint is completed. When a team member reports the progress of a task, the line moves up & down accordingly. Below is an example:

Sprint Goals

The Sprint Goal(s) are a set of goals which the team can meet by implementing items from the Project Backlog, and they exist to help the team understand why they're working on those particular items, and how they should be implemented.

Sprint goals are the outcome of cooperation between the development team and product owner. Scrum concentrates on goals resulting in product that is testable.

Sprint Planning Meeting

The Sprint Planning Meeting is where everyone decides on the work to be done during the Sprint.

Basically, this is a conversation between the product owner and the team. It should last no longer than eight hours, and is usually much shorter. The Scrum Master is in charge of making sure it takes place.

The goals of the Sprint Planning Meeting are twofold:

1. Decide what is achievable in the upcoming Sprint – which Product Backlog Items should be implemented, and what should the Sprint Goals be?

2. How will those Goals be achieved?

Sprint Retrospective Meeting

During the Sprint Retrospective Meeting, the Scrum team has a chance to consider itself as an organization and plan to improve during the upcoming Sprint. The focus is not on the product or Product Backlog, but rather on the team's way of working.

This meeting takes place at the end of each sprint immediately after the sprint-review-meeting. By the end of the Sprint Retrospective Meeting, the team has improvements to implement during the next Sprint.

Sprint Task

In Scrum, this is a section of work between four to fifteen hours.

Members of the Team volunteer to perform tasks and update the remaining work on a daily basis, in turn affecting the sprint burn down chart. The backlog items control tasks.

Team

There are two teams commonly spoken of in Scrum – the Scrum team, and the Development team.

The Development team are the ones who actually do the work of getting Product Backlog items "done."

The Scrum team consists of the Development team, plus the Product Owner and Scrum Master.

As a rule a Scrum Development team consists of 7 minus 2 or plus 2 people.

In a software development project, members of the development team are mix of architects, programmers, engineers, analysts, testers, QA experts, UL designers and so on.

Team member

In Scrum zone, a team member is anyone who works on a sprint task to meet the goal of the sprint.

Velocity

Velocity is the amount of product-backlog-effort a team handles in a single sprint.

Often, velocity is considered in terms of preceding sprints, assuming the sprint duration and team composition is kept constant.

When velocity is established, it can be utilized in planning projects and forecasting the completion dates of products.

Your Ultimate How-to-Use-Scrum Guide

To implement Scrum on any project, start by understanding Scrum's core principles.

These principles form the core guidelines for applying the Scrum framework to any project.

You should note that every project you undertake using Scrum should follow these principles.

Quick and Simple Ways to Understand Scrum: Basic Scrum Principles

In total, there are six Scrum principles that every project should follow. Let us start with the first one:

First Principle: The Empirical Process Control Principle

All Scrum decisions are based on experimentation and observation rather than meticulous planning before the project implementation.

The 'Empirical process control principle' relies on three key ideas to work well. These are inspection, transparency and adaptation.

Transparency

In a Scrum project, anyone involved in the project should be able to monitor all facets of the project.

Transparency means the creation of a clear and precise mechanism through which information within Scrum teams and the entire organization can be shared and viewed by anyone involved.

Decisions which result in increasing value and reducing risk are based on the decision maker's perception of what's going on. The greater the level of transparency, the more accurate and sound is the basis for those decisions.

Since Scrum is essentially decentralized – Scrum Development teams are self-organizing, with no hierarchy – transparency is crucial.

Scrum, in general, creates an open work culture.

Common aspects of Scrum transparency include:

Project vision statement

Release planning schedule

Prioritized product backlog

Meetings; daily standup meetings

Sprint review meetings

Information radiators; burn down chart

Scrum board

Inspection

The idea of inspection is that members of the Scrum team should frequently inspect the work and its progress in order to spot "undesirable variances" – potential problems, or minor problems which risk becoming major ones.

Scrum inspection might happen through:

- Use of a general Scrum board and other information radiators
- Collecting feedback from customers and stakeholders during the process and creating a prioritized product backlog"
- Inspecting and approving deliverables by the product owner and customers in the validate and demonstrate process.

Adaptation

In Scrum, adaptation occurs as the core team and stakeholders' team learn through inspection and transparency, thus improving the work they are doing. Adaptation is depicted through:

- Constant risk identification

- Daily stand up meetings

- Change requests

- Scrum guidance body

- Retrospective sprint meeting

Second Principle: The Principle of Self Organization

In a Scrum project, it's assumed that employees are self-motivated and are ready for greater responsibilities.

It's also assumed that they will deliver on these expectations when they are self-organized.

Some of the self-organization benefits are;

- Motivation, which leads to higher team performance

- Team buy-in, shared ownership

- Creating an environment that leads to optimal growth

Therefore, the Development team is self-organizing. Nobody can tell them how to turn Product Backlog Items into a potentially releasable product.

Furthermore, the Development Team should be cross-functional. The Team should have all the skills needed for a given Sprint and its Goals.

The Development Team members all have the same job title –
normally Developer. This is regardless of the work the person
actually does.

There are no sub-teams inside the Development Team, no
matter what work is involved.

The Development Team as a whole is accountable for the work,
no matter whether particular team members have specialized
skills.

Third Principle: The Principle of Collaboration

In Scrum, collaboration means members of the Scrum team
work together and cooperate with stakeholders to achieve
project goals that lead to achievement of the project vision.

The collaboration core dimensions are as follows:

- Awareness- Teams working together should be aware of
  each other's work

- Articulation- Collaborating teams should divide work
  into units, and then divide these units among team
  members. Later the work is re-integrated.

- Appropriation-When adapting a technology to one's own
  situation, the technology might be used in way that's
  completely different from what the designer intended.

Fourth Principle: The Principle of Value Based Prioritizing

Prioritizing is determining the order of work to be done:
separating what must be done right now and what needs to be
done later.

In Scrum, value based prioritizing is used as a principle to drive
the functionality and structure of the entire Scrum framework.

While prioritizing in the Scrum project, you should consider the
following.

- Value

- Risk or uncertainty

- Dependencies

Fifth Principle: The Principle of Time-Boxing

In Scrum, time is assumed to be one of, if not the the top most constraint while managing a project.

To address this constraint of time, Scrum uses a concept called time boxing, which guides the allocation of certain amounts of time to each activity in the Scrum project process.

The idea is simple enough: a time-box is a time limit which may not be exceeded. The time-box defines the time limits of meetings or development increments.

This assures Scrum team members do not take too much time or too little time performing their duties.

Time boxing has the following benefits:

- Efficient development process

- Less overhead

- High velocity for the team

Sixth Principle: The Principle of Iterative Development

Scrum focuses on the goal of delivering maximum business value in minimal time. To attain this goal, Scrum focuses on iterative development of deliverables.

The iterative model is highly effective in ensuring that any change of product requested by the customer can be easily included as part of the project.

Among its other benefits are:

- It enables better understating of what needs to be delivered as part of the project hence allowing for course correction

- It greatly reduces the time and effort required to reach the end of product development, and the team creates deliverables that are suitable to the final business environment.

Together, the elements of Transparency, Inspection, and Adaptation produce iterative development.

Transparency permits Inspection. When Inspection identifies an "unacceptable deviation," Adaptation means a correction will occur in the next iteration. (Or, if possible, sooner!)

How to Implement Scrum in 6 Easy, 20 Minutes-or-Less Steps

Implementing Scrum to a project can sometimes seem daunting.

It does not have to be.

In fact, it is possible to implement Scrum in 20 minutes or less.

I know what you're thinking "Is it really that easy and what does it take to implement Scrum to a project?"

The answer to your question is yes. Yes, implementing Scrum can indeed be easy (if you adhere to everything we have looked at thus far).

On the other question: what does it take to implement Scrum on any project?

The answer is six steps. Let's outline these six steps guaranteed to get you started fast.

Step#1: Choose A Product Owner

In any Scrum implementation, the first step is to identify a product owner who takes the responsibility of creating and prioritizing the product backlog.

The product owner should take ownership of the product backlog. As indicated earlier, only a product owner is in charge of prioritizing the product backlog.

Step#2: Create The Product Backlog

This step needs a lot of care.

Before you complete it, you need to understand the size (in either time or "story points" terms) of the product backlog items.

The amount of work involved will obviously have a major impact on decisions about priorities.

From a management point of view, this step also helps decide how big a Scrum team should be.

Step#3: Decide On The Sprint Budget

Your next priority should be deciding the teams sprint budget, both in time and money terms.

This will give you an idea of the number of hours available and required for the team to work on a sprint.

An easy way to create the sprint budget is by multiplying the available hours for the sprint duration by the number of full-time people working on the sprint.

In case there are people working part-time, include their hours as well.

Then deduct any time that the Scrum team will not work on the sprint.

Step#4: Plan Your Sprint Carefully

In this step, ensure that every member in the development team attends the sprint-planning meeting.

Based on the sprint budget, choose the Product Backlog Items which should be part of the Sprint Backlog.

Then, decide the duration each sprint should last. Remember that according to Scrum rules, sprints last less than 30 days. (This is for very good reason – above this time, things tend to get unmanageable in the context of the Scrum framework.)

Step#5: Build a Collaboration Hub for Your Team

One easy way to do this is to assign a whiteboard area representing the collaboration hub for your development team.

Let your team use this space to discuss and give feedback concerning the product process.

Also, use this place to stick things like ideas, high level plans, reports, posters, designs, etc.

Step#6: Prepare a Daily Burn Down Chart

A daily burn down chart is one of the most effective tools in any Scrum project.

Basically, it's used to track daily progress in the Scrum agile development framework. It's usually so useful that it represents a formidable competitor to any traditional project status report.

That's it!

Using the above six steps, the implementation of Scrum to any project becomes easy and almost effortless.

Now, with everything we have looked at thus far, you may be wondering, "Is it possible to use Scrum to rescue my projects?"

The answer is yes. In the next part, we will look at how you can do this.

How to Rescue a Project with Scrum: The Delicate Art of Adopting Scrum And Saving Projects

You may think of adopting Scrum to rescue your failing project as a drastic, frantic measure.

It's not... if executed properly.

Projects move to the Scrum framework for any number of reasons.

It might be because the project is in the analysis phase, and Scrum seems best.

It also may be that the project long-term mission is hairy and difficult, the project is not delivering the desired results, there is lack of transparency, etc.

In this case, the switch to Scrum might indeed happen "midstream."

So, how can you save your projects with the Scrum framework? The answer is simple, by using the following best practices:

Talk About the Benefits of Using Scrum, Not How Cool It Is

When introducing Scrum to your team and stakeholders, talk more about the benefits Scrum brings to the table in terms of project development and completion.

Highlight benefits such as:

- Incremental or continuous delivery- Mention sprints and how sprints will steadily improve the project. Mention that there will be a continuous working product every (period of time) and the customers will be impressed.

- Clarity or transparency: given that there are product backlog meetings where everyone will discuss and have access to each other at any time, it will be very easy to know what is happening.

- Control: product owners can modify the backlog contents continuously and can still hold teams accountable for setbacks in case the work product is not up to standard.

Hire an Expert to Lessen the Pain and Maximize Return on Investment

The role of a Scrum expert is similar to that of a Scrum master.

The duty of the coach or the expert is to make sure the roles, artifacts, and practices of the Scrum framework are followed. The expert will be there to offer a teaching role and a facilitate a "Scrum learning mode" for the project.

Compared with designating an in-house Scrum master, however, there's one key difference: the expert has experience in wide variety of situations.

This means that when things get tough, they know immediately how to handle the situation.

For a project that is already having trouble, this may make all the difference.

Carry Out a Workshop For Scrum Training

Introducing something new to your team is never easy.

The initial step is training them. Remember that Scrum can be initially difficult to understand and implement. Therefore, to deploy it, it might help to hold a workshop to train your team. There are companies that will do this for you. A tip: make sure that any formal external training has something like a case study exercise for the team to get hands-on experience.

Also remember you will need any training to be supported by all stakeholders. If you don't have buy-in, don't expect to get anything done.

Set Up Space for the Team

Scrum needs day-to-day fast, intense, paced meetings as well as four hour sessions in between sprints.

This means you will require a space and time where deliberations will take place and probably a product blog which should be kept updated continuously.

Make sure your team space is easily reachable by everyone involved!

Have a Solid Acceptance Criterion for User Stories

User stories (or in a larger sense, product backlog items) are the basis of creating workflow processes and sprint tasks.

Therefore, it's important that the Product Owner's criteria for accepting and rejecting user stories are clear and transparent.

This helps everyone avoid miscommunication and wasted effort.

Make the Product Backlog Prominent and Visible

Everyone's expectations for the project and the product and sprint backlogs should be located in a conspicuous location.

By doing this, it's easy for the team to see and check which product backlog items still need to be done – both during the sprint and in the project as a whole.

Design the backlog (however you represent it) in a way that it clearly flows from work to be done now to work to be done in the future.

Common Scrum Mistakes to Avoid At All Costs

Scrum is the most popular agile framework but it is also the most abused.

As we have seen, Scrum is simple in concept but it can be difficult to do well. Below are some common Scrum mistakes and what you can do to avoid them.

Expecting The Change to Agile/Scrum to be (Too) Easy

Anyone can pick up a book on Scrum, chop up requirements into user stories, hold some meetings, develop software in a 1-2 week sprint, then declare themselves a Scrum pro.

However, it's not necessarily that easy.

Especially in more complex situations, it's normal to encounter problems while making the change.

Someone who has a minimal level of experience with Scrum might be able to deliver working software.

However, how long do you think the run of good luck will last?

It's not until the initial glamour has faded in memory, teams are fighting hard to keep up with the pace, and software does not meet users expectation that things are really put to the test.

At this point, it's easy for the neophyte's well-intentioned efforts to look like a failure.

But, not to worry.

If you anticipate the challenges, you can prepare to meet them. Scrum transformation will always take time.

Often, it starts out messy. Real Scrum transformation exposes the existing culture and corporate problems that need be resolved.

Some of these problems are lack of accountability, poor communication, distrust, and more.

As a result, the most effective Scrum transformation often means a total culture change.

Therefore, make sure you give your Scrum implementation time. Be ready to experience pain and resistance, and make sure you have backing "from the top" as appropriate.

Practicing Without Adhering To the Principles

When implementing Scrum, holding meetings, using proper Scrum artifacts and filling Scrum roles is good.

However, did you know this is just half of the battle?

The other half of the battle is actually following the principles we outline earlier.

Unfortunately, many organizations fall short in this respect. Implementing the mechanical techniques without understanding why they're being implemented is a recipe for frustration and subsequent failure.

Scrum is, in the end, all about people's interactions and culture. Practices, processes, and tools are helping hands, but they can only help – not do it for you.

Complicating the Scrum Startup Process

Try as much as you can to keep the Scrum startup process simple.

Scrum will successfully work without the latest and coolest collaboration tool.

Spending precious time to get a tool up and running rather than getting people to work together is the wrong focus for your time and energy.

The Scrum framework focuses on individuals and interactions rather than on tools and processes for a reason. Keep it as simple as possible (but no simpler) and put your people first.

Communicating Through the Scrum Master

A common mistake on a new Scrum team is using the Scrum master as a messenger.

For instance, when a certain developer/ team member needs to know something about a user story, instead of asking for clear information from the product owner, he/she emails the Scrum master for more information.

This is wrong and must be avoided at all costs.

Scrum's main goal is enhancing communication and making it as direct as possible.

The time wasted in using a messenger is better spent getting an answer from the product owner or stakeholders.

You should strive to overcome the culture of indirect communication before it causes miscommunications among Scrum teams and team members.

Conclusion

Thank you again for downloading this book!

I hope this book was able to help you understand what you need to do to get up and running with Scrum.

The next step is practice. Give yourself time to change to the Scrum framework and focus on attaining your team set goals. Work towards following everything we have learnt, try to avoid some of the common mistakes we have looked, be consistent in the implementation of Scrum and you shall achieve your desired results regardless of the scope of your project.

Finally, if you enjoyed this book, would you be kind enough to leave a review for this book on Amazon?

Click here to leave a review for this book on Amazon!

(If that link doesn't work for you – try this one.)